Meet the Howlers!

Meet the

Papa

Mama

Howlers!

April Pulley Sayre
Illustrated by Woody Miller

Brother

Baby

Sister

ini Charlesbridge

Meet the howlers!
Living life on the go.
Meet the howlers!

Woo-hoo-hoo!

AH-UH-OH!

Howler monkeys are named for their incredibly loud calls, which can be heard a mile away. Only adult male mantled howler monkeys can actually howl. Infants make quiet "play calls," and young males yip or squeak.

Baby hitches rides
on his mama's fur.
But no one says he's lazy
or too big for her.

For its first few weeks, an infant howler monkey clings
to its mother. It holds on to her belly as she moves
through the treetops, feeding, climbing, and leaping.

Brother bounces branches,
leans and leaps—midair!
Yet no one nags, "Come down!
You're gonna fall from there!"

Howler monkeys live peacefully in forests with spider monkeys, capuchins, tamarins, sloths, and other forest creatures. But as the noisy howlers travel through the trees, they sometimes startle other animals, which climb or fly away.

Sister claims a branch,
yet no one says to share.
She never has to bathe.
Her suit is wash-and-wear!

Frequent rains wash
a howler monkey's coat.
Howlers sometimes nibble and
handpick insects, dirt, and leaves
out of their own and one another's fur.

Why?

'Cause these are howlers!
Furry, head to toe.
These are howlers!

Woo-hoo-hoo!

AH-UH-OH!

Even an adult howler monkey may take two or three naps per day.

Howler monkey faces may look glum, as if they are frowning. But that's just their regular, relaxed expression.

Brother rests a lot—
he hunches, lips curved down.
Yet no one ever asks him
if he's feelin' down.

Sister never waits
for breakfast, snack, or lunch.
She grabs a bunch of leaves
and gobbles—munch, munch, munch!

Howlers are unusual in that they eat lots of
leaves; most monkeys do not. Howlers also
eat flowers and fruit.

They play out in the rain,
but no one calls them in.
They never brush their teeth
or scrub their chinny-chins!

Howler monkeys live in tropical forests where it rains a lot. So being "out in the rain" is part of daily life.

Why?

'Cause these are howlers!
Climbing to and fro.
These are howlers!

Woo-hoo-hoo!
AH-UH-OH!

They never go to school
or learn their ABCs.
They lounge up in the arms
of the cecropia trees!

Howler monkeys live in groups of ten to twenty.
Babies are born at different times of year,
so a single group may have young howlers
of various ages.

If you ever get too close,
they will let you know.
Howlers send a special message:

Go, go, go!

When howlers sense that another animal, such as a person, is too close to them, they respond. They often urinate close to or on the invader to mark their territories. They may also call, shake branches, or drop fruit, leaves, or twigs on an invader.

Listen to their papa
growl and howl and bay.
Other howlers hoot
from treetops far away.

At dawn and dusk, adult male howler monkeys woof, grunt, bark, and howl. Each group of howler monkeys announces where it is and claims its territory. In this way, different families avoid fighting over places to feed and rest.

Why?

'Cause these are howlers!
Furry, head to toe.
These are howlers!

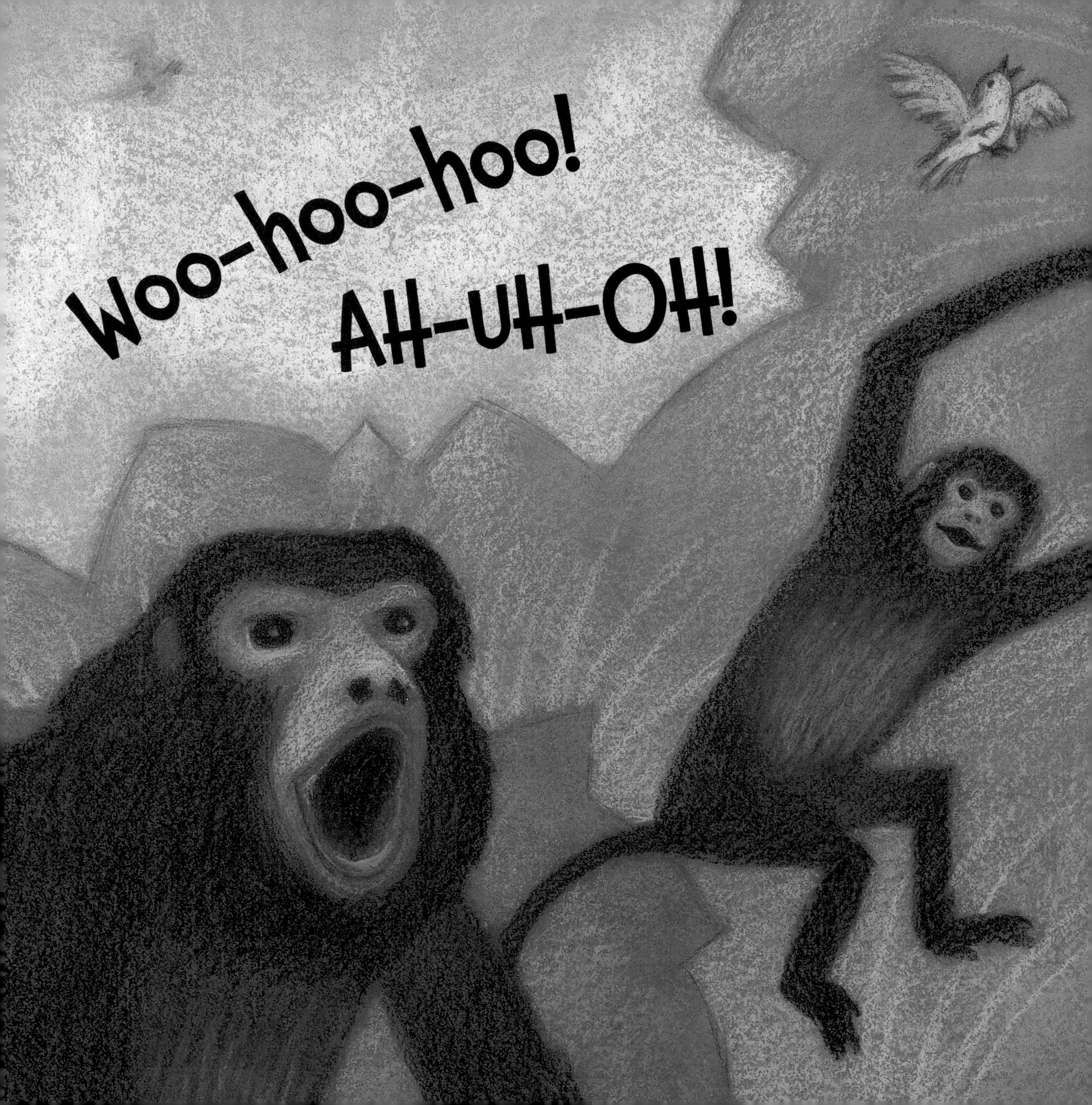
Woo-hoo-hoo!
AH-UH-OH!

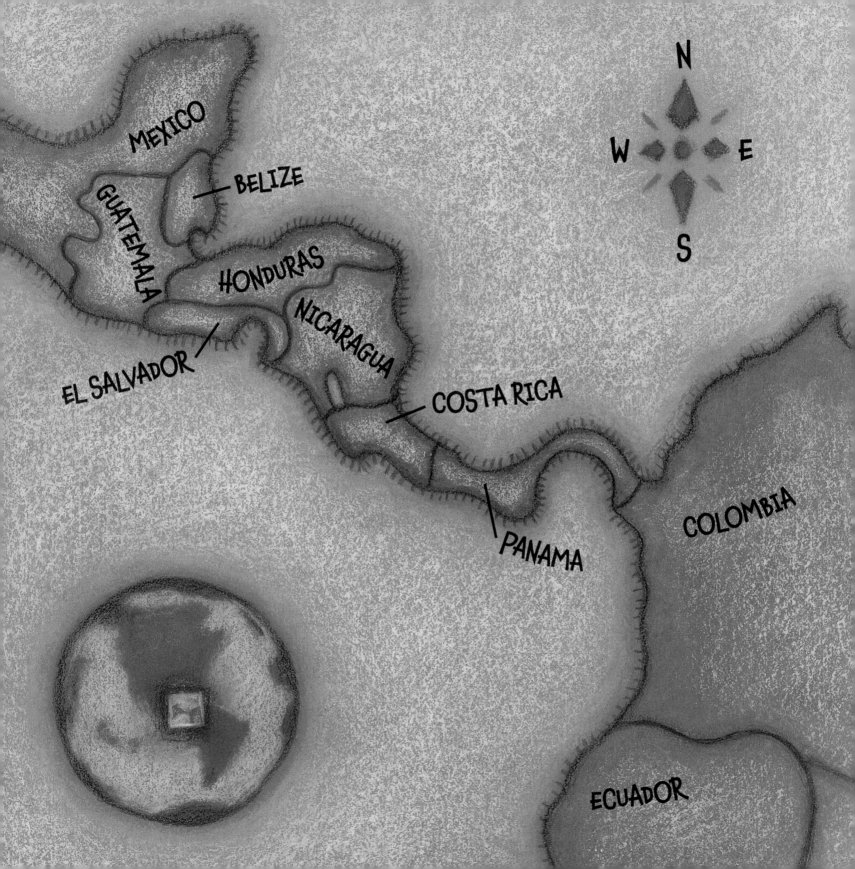

More about Howler Monkeys

Adult weight: 7–19 pounds

Life span: Wild adults live 7–12 years on average, but can live as long as 20 years

Range: Mantled howler monkeys *(Alouatta palliata)* live in tropical rain forests, dry forests, mangrove forests, and cloud forests in Mexico, Belize, Guatemala, Honduras, Nicaragua, Costa Rica, Panama, Colombia, and parts of Ecuador. Five other species of howler monkeys inhabit Mexico, Central America, and South America.

- Male howlers can't howl until they are fully grown, at four or five years old.

- A howler monkey's tail is prehensile, meaning it can grasp. A howler's tail can hold its entire body weight.

- Female howlers other than the mother howler may help take care of a baby. A sister, for instance, might make her body into a bridge to help the infant climb across a gap between trees.

- Cecropia (Si-KRO-pee-ah) are fast-growing trees. They often grow on the edges of forests or in sunny spots where trees have fallen. Their fruits are eaten by monkeys, birds, and bats.

- Howlers help plant trees! They eat many fruits with small seeds. The seeds travel unharmed through their digestive system and end up in their droppings. Dung beetles roll up the droppings and bury them in the soil. The seeds are deposited, complete with fertilizer (the rest of the dropping). As howler monkeys travel through the forest, their droppings are spread far and wide. So the seeds, and the trees, spread to new places.

For John David, who has a talent for figuring out things—A. P. S.

For Jessica. I couldn't monkey around without you!—W. M.

Acknowledgments
The facts in this book rely on the hard work of scientists, such as howler researcher Ken Glander, who was my professor when I studied primates at Duke University. My thanks to Carlos Bethancourt, who often guides us to see howlers and other wonders near Panama's Canopy Tower, and to Raúl Arias de Para, for establishing the lodge and encouraging ecotourism and conservation. My thanks also to Winston, Turner, and Nora, who were there when all this started.

Published by Charlesbridge
85 Main Street
Watertown, MA 02472
(617) 926-0329
www.charlesbridge.com

Library of Congress Cataloging-in-Publication Data
Sayre, April Pulley.
   Meet the howlers! / April Pulley Sayre.
      p. cm.
   ISBN 978-1-57091-733-2 (reinforced for library use)
   ISBN 978-1-57091-734-9 (softcover)
  1. Howler monkeys—Juvenile literature. I. Title.
QL737.P915S29 2010
599.8'55—dc22   2009003953

Printed in Singapore
(hc) 10 9 8 7 6 5 4 3 2 1
(sc) 10 9 8 7 6 5 4 3 2 1

Illustrations done in acrylic with watercolor crayon and colored pencil on Bristol paper
Display type and text type set in Chaloops by Chank
Color separations by Chroma Graphics, Singapore
Printed and bound September 2009 by Imago in Singapore
Production supervision by Brian G. Walker
Designed by Martha MacLeod Sikkema